Vegan Babies First Foods

Quick and Easy Meals and Purees for
a Healthy and Happy Vegan Baby

Project Vegan

Table of Contents

Intro

If you know the amazing results veganism can produce by following the lifestyle yourself, or maybe seeing the positive changes in one of your friends. You probably can't wait to share the benefits of veganism with your baby. Well your in luck! Veganism is just as healthy for babies as it is for adults. In fact, the Academy of Nutrition and Dietics have deemed a plant based diet healthy at any age, including throughout infancy. Although, just as when weaning your baby with any other diet, you'll need to be very strict with what you feed your baby to insure he/she is of perfect health.

You need to be careful to not exclude nutrients only found in certain foods, in particularly, you should try to incorporate foods with vitamin D, calcium and vitamin B12, as these nutrients are primarily only found in animal foods. Just like with any diet. It will take patience, and trial and error to perfect. This books goal is to highlight the most healthy and nutritious recipes for your baby, from their first puree to their first vegan burrito, as well as when and how to introduce fruits, veggies and other harder to ingest foods and how to make delectable delights that even the most picky eaters will enjoy.

Chapter 1: Breaking vegan parenting myths

Here are the most common misconceptions about a vegan diet for toddlers. Remember that you will need to adjust overtime and each babies dietary needs are unique, so make sure you educate yourself as much as possible on what will work best for your little one.

Myth 1: your body needs milk and dairy to build strong bones.

It is a fact that milk contains calcium, however the reason for this is because a cows diet consists of corn and soy that is fortified with calcium. As a vegan you can get calcium straight from the source simply by eating plant based foods that are calcium rich (such as dark leaf greens or soy based foods) as a result, you will also avoid the excessively bad fats, as well as cholesterol, antibiotics and hormones included in dairy. Take note also that Vitamin D aids your body in breaking down calcium, so be diligent on making sure your baby gets around 10 minutes of daily sunshine. On cloudy days you can take a vitamin D multi-vitamin.

Myth 2: Children need meat, fish or poultry to build strong muscles.

"Where will you get your protein" is probably one of the most repetitive and annoying questions people ask vegans on a daily basis. But keep in mind no mater how irritating this can be, the question merits a cohesive reply and attention as misinformation on topics like this have lead many people away from a vegan diet.

Requirements for protein will vary based on your little ones weight and age, but do not worry too much, as long as you are including protein rich foods such as beans, tofu, lentils, nuts and peas in most meals you're child will be as healthy as he/she can possibly be!

Myth 3: Vegan diets are dangerous for children, because meeting their nutritional requirements on a daily basis is unrealistic.

You will be hard pressed to find a medical doctor who can backup such claims about a vegan diet using any real evidence. In fact, the Academy of Nutrition and Dietics has found that following a well planned vegan diet alongside proper supplementation is very safe and beneficial to a infants health. This is one of the top nutrition authorities in the world, how is that for a stamp of approval?

So how do we put a plan into place? After all it's simple to become overwhelmed by macro counting proteins or calcium grams, as well as keeping track of the calories for each stage of your babies development. It's best to take it step by step and try to adjust as needed in the beginning.

Chapter 2: How you should feed a baby on a vegan diet

The first form of food a baby should have is breast milk. Some of the benefits of beast feeding babies include improving the immune system, as well as lowering risk of allergies and infection. Additionally, breast milk contains essential compounds developing infants require, which cannot be found anywhere else, including infant formulas. If you decide to breast feed, make sure you are getting a sufficient amount of B12, as it is essential for your babies health when breast feeding.

What foods you should eat while breast feeding

Pay close attention to getting a sufficient amount of calories as well as protein everyday wile breast feeding your little one. Plant foods are so calorically dilute, that you need to be sure you are not only eating until you are satiated, but also meeting your caloric needs as a breastfeeding mother. Remember you are eating for two after all.

What nutrients are most important to Vegan Infants?

Protein: Protein is the main compound that aids in growth, so it is of up most importance for your child during his/her greatest time of growth, which are the first two years. However it must be taken in very moderate amounts, ideally through breast milk. The protein in breast milk is contained by a mere 5% of the calories, this low level of protein is not found in unrefined plant based sources such as vegetables and starches since these foods have much bigger levels of protein. Making Breast an irreplaceable source of nutrition for infants.

Iron: Iron fortified foods such as rice cereal are a great first food for babies after they are finished breastfeeding. Aside from that, you can make your own formulas from scratch by pureeing foods like squash, yams, peas, carrots, well cooked beans, whole grains and tofu. Most raw fruits and vegetables are also great introductory foods. And if your toddler is less than 12 months old, pureed fruits and vegetables are especially a good choice.

Fiber: Foods high in fiber are very satiating and make children feel full before they get their daily recommended caloric intake by unrefined vegetables and starches. These foods have much higher levels of protein, for example, the protein content in sweet potatoes is 6%, beans 28%, and rice 4% respectively.

Omega 3's: During childhood, the brain is one of the fastest growing parts of the body. Plants are the only source of food that can synthesize basic essential fats the brain (omega 3's and 6.) A common misconception is that animals are the only ones that can elongate plant based building blocks and turn them into fats (such as DHA and EPA) however, infants are also efficient in doing the same, and no source of animal derived fats are needed to help.

Chapter 3: What foods do babies like?

Every parent has horror stories of their toddlers having a blast at your expense by redecorating the wall, ceiling, floor or even you and your clothing! It can even be difficult to predict what your little one will like, even if he/she favored it once in the past. Just be patient and things will work themselves out, this is just part of the territory when raising a child and you will persevere in the end. Here are some tips that will encourage your baby to eat a variety of foods and nutrients to get over being picky about what's on the plate.

Use timing to your advantage

A good time to try new foods is when your baby is most hungry, most of the time that is the first dish of the day, right in the morning. Try to take advantage of this moment to add in more varied and nutritious foods that your baby might otherwise reject.

Add a hint of sweetness

Humans have a ingrained liking for sweetness (hence why we have a "sweet tooth") mix in some sweet fruits or a sweet potato into non-sweet foods such as green vegetables and starches. But stay away from processed sugars since your baby's first food has the potential to influence their future preferences, even into adulthood. As a rule, it is best to stay away from processed sugars all together, especially overtly sweet packaged baby foods like pre-packaged juices or purees

Don't give up

If your baby just won't give in to certain foods, that's totally fine. Hold out on that particular food so your toddler is ready when it's time to try different newer foods once he/she has had enough of the same old routine. Don't beat yourself up over feeding your toddler the most healthy foods possible. Keep the experience fun and relaxed, and as long as your baby sticks to a variety of whole foods, your baby will be perfectly healthy and you will have nothing to worry about!

Chapter 4: Foods for every stage

This chapter will go a wide selection of healthy vegan recipes for your introductory feeding regimen. You can get very creative with how you approach this process. However these are my recommended food choices for feeding toddlers through the specific stages and how to prepare them

Note: Storing foods for later

After you've completed any of the following recipes, you can store in a fridge for up to 2 days. If there is too much food and your baby will not finish in 1 or 2 days, you can freeze the food in separate pieces. Place the food in a ice cube tray and freeze it, next remove the cubes and store in a gallon bag or container. Tag the bag/container accordingly and date and use anytime within 3 months.

4-6 Months

The introductory foods given to a baby are knows as **stage 1** baby foods. They are mostly pureed or mashed so your toddler can gulp them down effortlessly. However there is no guarantee your baby will react well to any of the foods that follow these guidelines, so make sure to consult the opinion of a pediatrician prior to feeding any new food to your little one.

Peach, pear and apple puree

Ingredients

1/3 Cup peaches, skinned, cored and chopped

1 Cup apples, peeled, seeded and chopped

1 Cup pears, skinned, cored and chopped

2 Tbsps of water

Directions

Put chopped peaches, pears and apples in a cooking pan and add the water. Cook to a boil than lower the heat until fruit is softened around 10 minutes. For a more creamy consistency, purees with a potato masher.

Apple, blueberry and Banana puree

Ingredients

1 Apple, skinned and diced

50 Grams blueberries

1 Tablespoon apple juice

1 Ripe and Spotted Banana

Directions

Put the apple pieces in a saucepan and add in the apple juice. Cover for two minutes as it simmers. Next add the blueberries for another 2 minutes. Add the banana pieces and cook for one more minute. Remove the mixture and puree in a blender. Serve.

Potato and zucchini puree

Ingredients

2 Cups zucchini, skinned and chopped

2 Cups veggie broth

2 Cups potatoes, skinned and diced

1 Tablespoon olive oil

S Teaspoon salt

Directions

In a pot, set water on high and cook potatoes until soft. In a sauce pan, saute the chopped zucchini in olive oil and add the salt. Cover and let sit on medium heat until fully tender. Remove both potatoes and zucchini and puree them in a mixer as well as the veggie broth. Serve right away.

Roasted Pear puree

Ingredients

3 Regular pears

j Teaspoon cinnamon

S Teaspoon vanilla

Directions

Pre heat oven to 400 F. Cut pears in halves and core the middle. Place pears bottom up in a non stick baking pan. Transfer to oven and bake for 20 minutes. Take out to cool and skin, then add all ingredients into a blender and mix until a smooth consistency is reached. Serve immediately!

Apple Puree

Ingredients

Apple

Water

Directions

Start by washing and peeling the apple and slice them into small chunks. Transfer the apple pieces to a pressure cooker. Add about 2-3 of water. Cook the apples for in the pressure cooker for 2 whistles. Place the pressure cooker under running water to cool down.

After the apple chunks are well cooked, place them in a blender and mix to a Puree, adding water to thin out the consistency.

Cauliflower and broccoli Puree

Ingredients

1 head cauliflower

Preheat the steamer, in the meantime, rinse the cauliflower and broccoli and lay out as florets.

Move to steamer and steam for around 10 or 15 minutes, until fully tender.

Puree the broccoli and cauliflower separately, adding hot water to achieve a soft texture. Serve as is.

Plum and beat root Puree

Ingredients

2 red plums, cut in half and cored
2 beetroot, skinned and chopped into small cubes

Directions

Move the plums and beetroot in a saucepan and fill with water.

Let cook to a boil on high then lower the heat, cover and simmer until the beetroot is tender, about 10-15 minutes.

Put the plums and beetroot in a mixer and blend until smooth.

Broccoli, tahini and pear puree

Ingredients

2 pears
1 broccoli head
3 tablespoons of tahini
Water

Directions

Preheat your steamer. Rinse the broccoli and spread into florets and transfer to steamer.

Skin and cut the pears into small pieces. Add to the steamer for around 10-15 minutes until food is tender.

After food is tender, transfer from heat and throw in the tahini and puree to desired consistency.

Let cool and serve.

Zuccini, pea and mint puree

Ingredients

2 zuccini

Handful of peas

1 tablespoon of finely chopped mint leaves

Water

Directions

Fill a pot with water and cook over medium heat and put the steamer above it and cook to a boil.

Cut the zuccini into chunks and move to the steamer with the peas.

Dash with mint and cook until the zuccini is tender, for around 10-15 minutes.

Puree and add boiled water to achieve a smooth consistency.

Apple and butternut squash

Ingredients

2 red apples

1 butternut squash

Dash of cinnamon

Directions

Preheat oven to 170 degrees.

Chop the butternut squash in half and remove the seeds.

Place the squash cuts face up in a cooking pan.

Skin and slice the apples and put them inside the squash. Dash with cinnamon

Bake in oven until the flesh is soft and tender, around 40 minutes

Take out the apples and squash and puree well, thinning out with water. Serve.

6-9 months

Crockpot Applesauce

Ingredients

2 Lbs butternut squash, skinned, cored and diced

3 Lbs apples, skinned, cored and sliced

S Tsp granulated cinnamon (optional)

j cup water

Directions

Note: Not all babies can tolerate spices before 12 months, so be careful if you are giving your baby spices for the first time.

Start by putting the squash and apples in the interior of the crockpot along with the nutmeg and cinnamon. Mix to finely coat and fill in with j cup of water. Cover to cook for around 5 hours on medium heat, once finished cooking you can drain any of the excessive liquid. Finally puree so the apple sauce is soft enough for your toddler.

Beets, blueberry and beats mash

Ingredients

2 Regular medium beets, cleaned well with water, skin and dice into chunks

S Cup frozen blueberries

Directions

Place the chopped/skinned beats into a saucepan with the blueberries. Fill with a sufficient amount of water so it covers the top of the blueberries and beets and cook for 10-15 minutes on medium, until beats are softened. Transfer into a blender and mix until smooth. Serve immediately.

Blueberry, Avocado and mango raw puree

Ingredients

S Cup blue berries

1 Thick slice of mango, skinned and chopped

1 Avocado

Directions

You can choose to puree with a fork until all fruit is gathered, so you get a chunky consistency or you can toss the mixture into a blender for 20 seconds to get a smooth consistency.

As with most avocado purees, this recipe is ideal if consumed a little while after done making.

Peach-Mango Puree

Ingredients

1 Mango, cored, skinned and sliced into chunks

1 Peach, pitted and chopped

1 or 2 Tablespoons unsweetened breastmilk or water

1 or 2 Tablespoons any baby cereal

Directions

Mix peach, mango and liquid into a blender until consistency is soft. Add in cereal, or if your baby cannot tolerate thicker foods you can choose to not add cereal at all. Serve as is or refrigerate if preferred.

Pumpkin and Thyme Mash

Ingredients

1 Small Pumpkin

S Cups Breast Milk or Water

1 Teaspoon fresh thyme

Directions

Preheat oven to 350 F. Put parchment paper over a baking sheet. Slice the top of the pumpkin, than cut in half from top to bottom, core out the middle until it's clean, but don't stress over removing the strings, as they will puree along with the pumpkin.

Dice the pumpkin into cubes and move to the baking sheet, make sure skins are fully removed. Bake for 50 minutes or until very tender. Remove from oven and let cool, once cool enough to handle. Put all ingredients into a blender and mix. If the consistency is not smooth enough, just add more water.

Serve as is or add to oatmeal, pancakes or any of the puree you see fit.

Pasta with Vegetables and Cheese Sauce

Ingredients

1 S cups dailya vegan grated cheese

1 S cups earth balance vegan butter

1 Tbsp Soy or Almond Milk

1 Tbsp Chopped Broccoli Florets

1 Cup Whole Flour

4 Cups Pasta

Directions

Cook pasta as the package advises. Chop broccoli florets into small chunks and steam I a pot until tender, around 10 minutes. In the meantime, in a skillet or saucepan, melt the vegan butter. Throw in the flour and stir well, gradually adding the vegan milk, stirring occasionally until the sauce is creamy. Add in the Daiya cheese and stir. Add the veggies and cooked pasta. Stir until gathered and serve hot or warm.

Pear and cinnamon oatmeal

Ingredients

1 cup oats

S cup soy milk

S cup water

1 pear, skinned, cored, grated dash of cinnamon

Directions

Place the oafs, milk and water in a pan and cook to simmer for around 5 minutes while constantly stirring. Remove mixture into a bowl and stir in the rest of the ingredients. Set aside to cool down and serve.

Potato, broccoli and pea puree

Ingredients

Black pepper

50g frozen peas

100g broccoli

Soy milk

Earth balance vegan butter

350g potatoes

Directions

Skin and dice potatoes, put the broccoli and the potatoes in a steaming basket for around 10 minutes.

Add in the peas at the last 3-4 minutes.

After all the veggies have tenderized, transfer to a bowl and puree well, adding seasoning and he vegan butter. Serve as is or with added breast milk, if you would prefer to thin this out for your baby.

9-12 months

Banana quinoa puree

Ingredients

S Ripe banana

Dash of cinnamon

3 Tablespoons quinoa

1 Tablespoon Daiya vegan yogurt

Directions

Put banana in a bowl and mash to puree. Throw in the remainder of the mix and stir in. Serve as is or refrigerate to cool.

Apple and apricot crumble

Ingredients

1-3 large sized apples

4-6 apricots, or S canned apricots

1 tablespoon cinnamon

3 tablespoons ground almond

30 grams organic sugar

50 grams Natures Balance vegan butter

150 grams white flour

Directions

Preheat oven to 220 F. Cut the apples into small pieces, then put in a skillet or saucepan, cover the apples with water and bring to a boil. Reduce the heat to a simmer and add cinnamon, stir often for 6 minutes or until the apples are tender. In the meantime, put the flour and vegan butter in a clean bowl and caress them until they have a flakey consistency, next add the sugar and stir.

Dice the apricots and core out the stones. Turn off the heat and stir in the apricot chunks, than transfer the mix into a baking dish. Layer with the crumble mixture and top off with crushed almonds. Put in the oven and cook for 30 minutes or until the top is golden brown coated. Set aside to cool before serving.

Tomato, carrot and cauliflower with basil

Ingredients

2 Medium carrots, skinned and chopped

2 Regular tomatoes, skinned, cored and finely diced

1 Cup cut cauliflower florets

2 Tablespoons unsalted vegan butter (any brand, vegan)

2-3 Basil leaves

S Cup grated Daiya vegan cheese

Directions

Put the carrots in a skillet or saucepan. Cover and add water and bring to a boil. Lower heat to a simmer and cook for 10 minutes, throw in the cauliflower florets and cover, cook for another 8 minutes. In the meantime melt the vegan butter in a separate pan, than throw in the tomatoes and cook on medium heat until mushy.

Remove the mixture and add in the vegan cheese and basil. Mash the cauliflower and carrots with the tomato sauce and about S cup of the leftover liquid.

Dried apricot puree

Ingredients

2 Cups any brand diced apricots

4 Cups all natural apple juice

Directions

Finely cut the fruit and mix with juice in a pan or skillet. Cook to a boil then lower the heat to simmer. Take mixture out of pan and let cool down before pureeing. Use water to puree to your desired consistency.

Sweet spinach

Ingredients

1 ripe banana

2-3 cups spinach

Directions

Fill pot with to around 1 inch depth and boil over medium heat.

Transfer spinach into a floating steamer basket and boil the basket in a pot, not letting the water contact the spinach.

Cover the pot and let simmer for around 6 minutes and mix until consistency is creamy and serve immediately.

Yogurt and beat puree

Ingredients

1 beet

2 cups any vegan variety milk and plain daiya yogurt.

Directions

Cut off the stems from the beats, rinse beats off using cold faucet water, skin and chop.

Fill a pot with water until about 2 inches are covered and cook to a boil.

Put beets in a mixer of your choice and puree until consistency is smooth. Set aside to cool and serve with yogurt topping.

Black beans with zuccini and corn

Ingredients

1/2 can of black beans, rinsed and drained

1 zuccini, rinsed and sliced

1 cup fresh or frozen corn

Directions

Pour around 1 inch of water into a pot and bring to a boil. Transfer the zuccini and corn into a floating steamer basket and transfer into the boiling pot, making sure the water does not have contact with the basket. Cover the pot and let simmer for 7 minutes.

Next place the zuccini and corn into a blender along with the black beans and mix until consistency is thick and chunky, but just soft enough that the baby can ingest with ease.

Muesli breakfast

Ingredients

15g oats

3/4 cup soy milk

5 dry apricots, softened in warm water

1 pear, skinned and chopped

Directions

Put oats and soy milk in a cooking pan, cook to a simmer for around 3 minutes until the puree is thick. Let cool and put in a mixer with the boiled apricots and chopped pears. Blend well until consistency is creamy and smooth

Mixed fruit muesli

Ingredients

1 tablespoon raisin

1 pear

1 hand full chopped raisins

Directions

Put the oats and milk in a bowl and soak overnight,
skin the pear and grate it into the rest of the mixture.
Stir in the raspberries and raisins and serve.

Rice pudding

Ingredients

S cup soy or breast milk

3 tablespoons rice

2 drops vanilla essence

Directions

Put the milk in a pan and heat until hot. Add in the rice and mix until the consistency is creamy and free of lumps. Turn off the heat and add in the vanilla and mix. Serve as is.

Mini pancakes with berry yogurt

Ingredients

s cups white flour

1 whole vegan egg replacer (any brand)

2/3 cups soy milk

1 tablespoon olive oil

1//4 cup daiya yogurt

1 fresh strawberry

2 fresh blueberries

2 fresh raspberries

Directions

Pour flour in a bowl. Add the milk and egg and whisk until batter mix is smooth. Next cook the oil over mid heat, stirring occasionally so the butter does not stick. Add a spoon of two of the mix about 1 minute, flip over to the other side and cook for half an hour. Finally mix the fruit with the yogurt and blend well.

Banana Dosa

Ingredients

1/2 cup mashed banana

1/2 cup dosa batter

1 or 2 teaspoon sugar

Earth balance vegan butter

1 teaspoon of date syrup

Preparation

Condition the spoons and bowls for your toddler in a compartment with hot water for 5 minutes and keep them there until use.

Directions

Mash bananas with a fork or your hand. Mix the dosa in with the bananas until texture is smooth. Set aside.

Heat up a skillet and add a small portion of banana dose batter and even it out to make a mini dosa, add a hint of the butter or oil. Cook on one side until brown, around 5 minutes. Let cook for another minute and take off of heat. Do the same for the rest of the mix.

Apple, parsnip and carrot mash

Ingredients

4 carrots

4 parsnips

4 apples

Dash of cinnamon

1 tablespoon olive oil

Directions

Skin and chop carrots, apples and parsnips and move them to a salad bowl with a dash of cinnamon and olive oil. Stir in well.

Transfer the mixture from bowl into a baking pan with some slight oil and cook at 400 degrees for around 25 minutes until foods are tender to a fork touch. Once done baking, set aside to cool and mash as needed.

Lentil, apple and sweet potato salad

Ingredients

3 medium sized sweet potatoes

1 regular sized apple

2 cups tablespoon olive oil

1 teaspoon cinnamon

Directions

Skin the sweet potatoes and chop into small cubes, skin core and chop the apple into small chunks. Add lentils and 2 cups of the broth or water to a boil in a pot. Lower the heat once the lentils start boiling. Continue to cook lentils on low heat for about 25 min until lentils have softened.

Add 1 cup of water to a separate cooking pot as well as in steam basket into it.

Add the diced apple and sweet potato chunks to the steaming basket and simmer for around 20 minutes, until sweet potatoes are softened.

After the sweet potatoes and lentils are cooked, move to a sink and drain any excess juice from the saucepots. Allow to warm.

After foods have warmed, mix the foods in a salad bowl with 2 tablespoons of olive oil. Add a dash of the spices and stir well.

Peachy sweet potatoes

Ingredients

1 sweet potato, skinned and chopped

2 fresh potatoes, cored and chopped

Dash of cinnamon ginger

Water

Directions

Merge peaches and sweet potatoes in a cooking tray with enough water to just cover the food. Garnish with a dash of cinnamon and stir. Cover the dish with foil. Cook for around 20 minutes until sweet potatoes and peaches are tender.

After fully cooked, save any left over water and move peaches and sweet potatoes to a bowl to cool. Puree to your babies desired preference and serve.

Final Words

Raising a vegan baby is very rewarding although it calls for efficiency and dedication. If you are a first time parent it may also be too overwhelming because there is not much time to learn from past mistakes when bringing up a baby, but I truly hope the information in this book has helped you overcome many of these hurdles.

Made in the USA
Lexington, KY
19 March 2018